The Ballet Buffet: Recipe for Success When Teaching Technique

Ballet Buffet Book One

Brenda Bobby

ISBN: 978-0-9861946-6-5
ISBN-10: 0986194662

DEDICATION

This, my first book, is dedicated to my four children: Tyler, Dylan, Ellie and Jack.

Over my 20-plus years at the studio developing these teaching skills, I was not always able to attend your little league games, basketball tournaments, or birthdays. You always supported my work, and I am proud of the independent, determined individuals you have become.

As I transition into this new professional journey, I hope that I can inspire you to never stop growing and evolving. Live life on your own terms, answer to yourselves, and remember, if your dreams and goals don't scare you, then you are not aiming high enough.

ACKNOWLEDGEMENTS

There are so many dance educators who have influenced and inspired me, but there are a few that have also given insight and support to help make this publication possible. Thank you, Duncan Cooper, Michelle Spezio-Ferm, Alexandra Brysden, Patty Neal, Francisco Gella, and all the educators with whom I have taken classes in the last 44 years.

I owe a huge thank you to my publisher, Jan Myers at LJM Publishing LLC,who really assisted and encouraged me in every step to make this idea come to fruition.

A big thank you also to my illustrator, Javier, who not only had to learn about ballet, but also make my crazy analogies become visual guides to the imagery in my mind.

Table of Contents

Introduction

Developing a strong ballet foundation is essential for long-term success in dance. I learned this first hand as a studio owner, working very hard to keep dancers interested in learning the basics and found analogies the best way to engage dancers. By relating the movement to food, students of all ages can easily understand and apply concepts to their movement.

I originally started using these analogies with young dancers; however, I found that even young adults and older dancers were interested in what we were doing. Everyone loves food treats, and the concepts serve as wonderful reminders of simple ideas that have been so repetitive for the seasoned dancer that the reason and initiation of the movement were sometimes forgotten.

The Ballet Buffet can be a good refresher course for those experienced dancers as well as a great introduction to the fundamentals for the beginner dancer. There are several ways to incorporate the concept of the Ballet Buffet into a school's program.

1. You may offer the Ballet Buffet as a workshop for at least two hours. Present concepts in a long ballet seminar that concludes with a Ballet Buffet feast of foods from the analogies presented in the seminar.
2. A second option is to introduce a new analogy each week and offer the "food" as a treat at the summation of class.
3. I also found the Ballet Buffet is a great way to introduce healthy treats, food choices, and alternatives for dancers. With childhood obesity at an all-time high, it's important to make food fun and healthy for children, so there are endless possibilities with this concept.

The Ballet Buffet: Recipe for Success When Teaching Technique

This book is the first in a series that will break down the basic exercises of a traditional ballet class starting at the barre, followed by center work in volume two, and across the floor exercises in the third book. The Ballet Buffet is for all levels of dancers at all ages. You are invited to use these ideas as a springboard to create new analogies and expand the buffet for all to enjoy!

Chapter 1 - Setting the Table: Warm Up

Posture Exercise: Table and Chairs

Chairs & Stools: In butterfly position, manipulate your body into a chair with a tall back and a round seat. Hold posture tall for eight counts. Next, follow this movement and create a stool by rounding forward for eight counts. Use verbal cues of a tall back chair so dancers can train and learn to lengthen their spine.

Banquette/Booth & Picnic Benches: In a straddle position, dancers sit tall with arms in the second position to represent the back of the banquette/booth and hold for eight counts. Next fold forward to create a flat picnic style bench for eight counts.

Folding Table: Dancers lay down on the floor with legs extended out long. Maintaining a long back with the lower back pressed toward the floor. The ribcage must be closed and shoulders connected to the floor while arms are extended. Hold the center and engage for eight counts. Advanced dancers may "fold their table" by coming up to a V position, while still maintaining a long line through their spine and legs, and then lowering back to the table position on the floor. The folding table exercise is a great core strengthening exercise.

Feet & Ankle Exercises: Cutlery

Knife, Spoon & Fork: With legs extended out in front long, and posture tall, dancers will create knives by pointing ankle and feet in full extension, holding for eight counts. Dancers may sit against the wall to maintain tall posture throughout this exercise. Next, dancers will flex their foot and ankle to create the "fork" for eight counts. After repeating this motion several times, dancers will circle the ankles for four counts in each direction creating the circle of the 'spoon.'

Port de Bras Exercises: Place Settings

Plates, Glasses & Napkins: This series can be done seated or standing. Start with arms extended and create a "plate" by rounding arms to first position, holding for eight counts. Ask dancers to "show the audience" the food on their plate, forcing them to automatically lower their hands so that the audience can see the "plate" in the mirror. Next, they will create a tall glass by raising their arms to fifth position for eight counts. Lastly, dancers will open their 'folded' napkin, by opening their arms from fifth to second position, holding for eight counts. Use verbal reminders such as support the undercarriage of their arms and keep elbows lifted, and as they open their arms, lengthen the back of the hand. This will create a long line and promote moving their arms from their backs.

Chapter 2 - Plié: Pliable, Cushy Movement

A plié is a defined movement or action in which a dancer bends the knee(s) and straightens them again. A "bent" or "soft knee" is not acceptable technique. The action of a plié is the most important movement in ballet as almost all ballet movement incorporates the plié. The idea of oppositional force and a steady and consistent center is both fundamental and critical to exercising crisp and clean form. To help dancers conceptualize oppositional forces and the idea of contraction and expansion, I use the 'marshmallow' as my sweet analogy to flavorful and divine plié.

The 'Marshmallow' Pliés: Think of your plié as a marshmallow! One must apply pressure to both the top and bottom of the marshmallow to make it smaller or to fit it in your mouth. As you squeeze the top and bottom of the marshmallow, it compresses while the sides expand, like the knees of a dancer widen as they plié.

As you release the pressure from the top and bottom of the marshmallow, it slowly returns to its original shape, much like the recovery of the plié. The oppositional concept of the plié is important to help dancers understand this movement is an action with energy and not a static movement. You may use mini-marshmallows to represent the demi-plié and large, campfire marshmallows to represent the grand-plié.

To help students train students on the importance of a plié, you can use s'mores as an example. The marshmallow is the critical ingredient in s'mores, holding all the other components together. Without the marshmallow, the chocolate and graham crackers would crumble and fall apart, much like a leap or turn would fall apart without using the plié to prepare and complete the movement. In this s'mores analogy, dancers are reminded to keep their pelvis and feet flat and engaged.

Chapter 3 - Tendu: Smooth like Butter

The definition of a tendu is stretched, as in the leg extends and stretches out from the supporting leg to a fully pointed foot. The foot stays connected to the floor the entire time when executing a tendu, and as you stretch the leg, you should be pushing against the floor to warm up and prepare your legs, ankle, and feet for more advanced skills. To get dancers to understand the idea of using the floor and pressing down as you lengthen out, I use the bread and butter analogy.

Bread & Butter Tendu: Think of the floor as a slice of bread (bagel, rice cake, etc.) and your leg as the knife spreading the butter (or peanut butter, almond butter, jelly, etc.). In order to cover the entire piece of bread, you have to apply pressure to the knife evenly across the entire piece of bread to get a nice even spread. If you don't press down as you are spreading your butter, you get big, uneven clumps (or holes) in your bread. Most dancers forget to "use the floor" in tendu exercises, which often leads to other exercises being performed incorrectly. It is also important to maintain turnout so the 'knife' should not flip or rotate inward.

Chapter 4 - Dégagé: Peeling your Apple

The definition of dégagé is to disengage. It is an extension of a tendu in which the foot leaves the floor slightly in a quick sweeping motion. If you use the bread and butter technique from the previous tendu exercise, dancers will already understand that they must use the floor and apply pressure to the ground by the working leg. To understand the rapid release of the foot from the floor in a dégagé, I use the idea of peeling the skin off an apple (or a fruit or vegetable) using a peeler.

Dégagé Apple Peels: When you peel an apple with a hand peeler, you start at the top and press firmly, swiftly and evenly all the way down the apple, and then release the peeler away from the apple to lift the skin off in one piece. The longer and more even the pressure, the more of the skin comes off in each stroke.

Using the floor as your 'apple' and your working leg as the 'peeler,' dancers push down as they extend the leg out until it disengages from the floor. As quickly and firmly as they can, bring the leg back in peeling away another layer from the apple in all directions until all the 'skin' is peeled away.

Chapter 5 - Rond De Jambe: Apple Slices

The definition of *rond de jambe* is a circular movement of the leg. To execute a proper rond de jambe, the working leg should create a semi-circle like the shape of an apple slice. Rond de jambe can be done a terre (touching the floor) or en l'air (in the air) and in both directions. For this particular movement, I chose the shape of the movement to match the food so the analogy can be used in all cases.

Ron De Jambe Apples: Using the apple concept from the previous exercise, we now are going to use the apple to make apple slices. The shape of an apple slice is the visual; dancers will create 'apple slices' by moving the working leg in a semi-circle, passing through first position each time. You can remind students that each slice needs to be 'cut' the same and as large as possible. Also, remind them not to get the 'seeds' in the slice, so they should not over cross the foot and hit the 'apple core.'

Chapter 6 - Frappé Kabobs

The definition of **frappé** is to strike, and the movement is done at the barre to improve quick, precise movements of the leg and foot. The working leg starts in a **coupé** position with either a flexed or pointed foot and, using the ball of the foot, the working foot strikes the floor as it extends out from the standing leg. I use the idea of kabobs (either fruit or meat and vegetable kabobs) as the analogy to demonstrate the 'striking' motion of a **frappé**.

Frappé shish kabobs (chicken on a stick):

Eating food on sticks is fun and quick, and so are **frappés**. Think of the floor as a piece of chicken (or beef, vegetables, or fruit), and you want to make a kabob to eat. Use the working leg and foot as your "stick" you have to strike or push through the piece of chicken (or other food choice) to get it on the stick. You have to push through the piece completely so that you can continue to add additional pieces to the kabab.

Chapter 7 - Fondu: The Melting Pot

The definition of fondu is to melt. While standing on one foot, you bend and extend both the working leg and standing leg in a slow and controlled movement. Although fondus are usually not introduced in a basic ballet class, the idea of fondu can be fun for older or more experienced dancers.

The Chocolate (or cheese) Fondue: Imagine a large pot that is heated and contains chocolate (or cheese if you prefer to use vegetables over fruit). Think of your working leg as a toothpick with a strawberry (or other fruit) on the end and you want to dip the fruit in the chocolate pot, slowly bending it in, and then slowly lifting it out so the chocolate doesn't make a mess everywhere.

Chapter 8 - Grand Battements: Ice Cream Scoops

The definition of a grand battement is a large moving of the leg. In a grand battement or a 'high kick,' one leg is thrust into the air while maintaining a strong and still-standing leg and posture. Getting dancers to brush from underneath then rotate (like in a 'J' or scooping position) without lifting the leg from the hip and quad is a common struggle. This occurs especially when a proper placed grand battement is not as high as the dancer would like, but I have found the ice cream scoop analogy especially helpful.

Grand 'Scoops' of Battements: Imagine the working leg as a big ice cream scoop and the floor as a gallon of ice cream (or frozen yogurt, sherbet, etc.). If the dancer wanted to get the biggest scoop of ice cream possible, they would dig down deep and rotate the scoop as it lifts out of the gallon. If you simply held the scoop from the front or merely lifted it straight up, it would not produce the LARGEST scoop you could get. This concept not only helps dancers use the floor and grip less in the quads but to actually rotate and extend the leg in a turned-out position that will help keep the hips down and posture stabilized.

Chapter 9 - At the Ballet (Buffet)

No matter how you decide to offer the Ballet Buffet Program, I find letting the kids enjoy the "treats" really helps them to make the connection and keep what sometimes is the dry repetition of ballet more exciting.

I have found the most cost-effective way to offer the program is to run it as an 'add on,' either during a school break, summer time, or as a great way to get new students throughout the dance season.

Offering it in a two-to three-hour seminar or 'intensive,' you can generate additional income, open it up to dancers outside your current client list, and budget for the food and paper products, etc. You can also do add-ons such as tutus with aprons, or have them dress up for the buffet dinner as though it's a formal event and incorporate manners and etiquette lessons.

Of course, creating recipe books for healthy dancers is an option, too. There are so many possibilities.

About the Author, Brenda Bobby

Brenda began dancing at the age of 3 when her pediatrician noticed how very naturally flexible her body was and encouraged her mother to enroll her immediately in dance class.

She grew up in a traditional, but competitive "tap" and "jazz" studio in Rochester, NY; however, she was told that "ballet is the foundation of dance," and that it was through ballet that one would become a well-trained dancer.

Since Brenda was born with banana feet, very open hips, and a gumby back, she didn't understand why everyone couldn't just do the things she could do, moving in a way she felt was so natural and easy. It wasn't until she started teaching that she realized not everyone had her natural flexibility and aptitude for ballet.

Brenda was fortunate to work with the late Timothy Draper during her teen and college years. Tim was a well-respected and important figure in Rochester dance and the community. He also became Brenda's friend and mentor. Not only did Tim help Brenda develop her movements, but he also taught her the methods behind the movements, and he trusted her as a teacher. In addition, Tim employed her while in college. Brenda credits Tim with helping to make her the teacher and person she is today.

Brenda graduated from State University of New York – Brockport with a Dance and Health Sciences BS, and it was then that she decided to open her own studio. Brenda founded and operated Pittsford Dance for 20 years, starting with just a single room dance studio that grew to a nationally ranked studio that combined raw talent and hard work to develop professional dancers.

Over more than 20 years of teaching, Brenda developed many unique and special methods to connect dance and acro movement to relatable activities with which children and young adults could identify, successfully beginning with toys and other sports.

And yet, Brenda knew she needed more, so she began broadening her horizons. She began attending The Dance Teacher Summit, Rhee Gold's Studio Owners' Retreat, Dance Teacher Expos, NYCDA's teacher intensives, BDC Summer Teacher Intensives. She took advantage of any and every learning opportunity that could provide her with insight, ideas, and strategies to make the mind-body connection easier and more fluid for teachers and students.

Over the years, Brenda's experience and thirst for knowledge led her to identify concepts and imagery from many resources that assisted her in bringing her own ideas and teaching aides to life.

- In 2012, Brenda became an adjudicator for Hall of Fame Dance Challenge, a national dance competition.
- In 2017, Brenda decided to expand her reach to more than just the students in Western New York. So she downsized her program in Pittsford, NY, and relocated to Miami, FL where she began teaching, consulting and connecting with dance and fitness professionals to further sharpen, refine and enhance her skills.
- Currently, Brenda runs a recreational program in Pittsford, NY, and works as an educator, consultant and adjudicator for national competitions, conventions, studios, and individuals.
- Through her travels, professional experience, and exposure to different cultures, studios, dancers, and teachers, Brenda created a formal series of educational tools that have assisted her and her students over the years.

All this Brenda accomplished while still making time to rear her four children.

Upcoming Books by Brenda Bobby

Watch for the Center and Across the Floor Editions, Ballet Buffet Pre-Fix, a menu and recipe guide, as well as other books to come!

Please go to BrendaBobby.com to sign up to be notified of the publication of each upcoming book.

Book Reviews

I hope you have found this spread of barre fundamentals informative and thought-provoking. If so, would you do me the favor of leaving a review on Amazon.com? I would really appreciate it.

Contacting Brenda Bobby

Email: BrendaBobby2018@gmail.com

Website: BrendaBobby.com

Click the Link Below to Download Your Free Coloring Sheets

http://brendabobby.com/downloadable-coloring-sheets-book1/

Made in the USA
Coppell, TX
29 August 2020

34748459R00019